BOY POWER

Virgin

First published in 1998 by Virgin Books
an imprint of Virgin Publishing Ltd
Thames Wharf Studios
Rainville Road
London W6 9HT

A catalogue record for this book is available from the British Library

ISBN 0 7535 0284 4

Printed and bound by Butler & Tanner, Frome and London.

Designed by Slatter~Anderson

Contents

Contents

Mark Owen	4
Brian Littrell	6
Damon Albarn	8
Lee Brennan	10
Leonardo DiCaprio	12
Kevin Richardson	14
Jamie Theakston	16
Matt Le Blanc	18
Aaron Carter	20
Matthew Marsden	22
Michael Owen	24
Nick Carter	26
Rich Neville	28
Ewan McGregor	30
AJ McLean	32
Robbie Williams	34
Ronan Keating	36
David Schwimmer	38
Shane Lynch	40
Howie Dorough	42
Taylor Hanson	44
Will Mellor	46

Mark Owen

It's hard to believe that Mark Owen spent most of his life suffering a major lack of self-confidence.

Let's face it, the former bank clerk from Oldham was the most popular member of Take That during their six-year reign as kings of pop — and he's sold more than two million records since going solo. But even at the peak of his fame, when he was voted Most Fanciable Male In The World by *Smash Hits,* he's said that he felt he was worthless and not as talented as the other guys. When the band split, Mark went the opposite way to his mate Robbie Williams, turning to spiritualism rather than drinking and partying as a way of coping with his new life. Like Robbie, he said he needed to prove that there was more to him than a nice haircut and a pretty face. Mark bought a house in a village in the Lake District and has changed his image from squeaky clean to grunge, and doesn't miss his boy band days much. He's said that the day Take That split up was the happiest day of his life.

He's said that the day Take That split up was the happiest day of his life.

The only regrets Mark has about his days in Take That is that the punishing dance routines knackered his knees, and the fact that he never had time for love. Now he has finally found a woman who he can rely on to nurse his aching knees — his art student girlfriend Joanne Kelly. 'I've known Jo for years, but I couldn't commit fully to a relationship until Take That had finished. It was only then that I was able to ask her to get a house together and stuff.

I love her dearly and I'm a lucky man.'

Brian Littrell

The Backstreet Boys just couldn't find their last member until Kevin Richardson came up with a brainwave and suggested his cousin Brian from Kentucky. He was already a hit with the local girls, who screamed for his fantastic voice every time he stood in front of a mike at school talent shows. So it came as no surprise on the day of his audition that it only took a few bars of singing to convince the group that he was their fifth member.

Brian nearly died as a baby because of a heart defect, and spent much of his childhood receiving medical treatment for his condition, but it didn't stop him from playing his much loved basketball — hence his nickname B-Rok — and learning to sing in church choirs. But the strain of Backstreet's punishing work schedule around the world eventually took its toll on Brian's health. Earlier this year he underwent surgery to help correct the hole in his heart but he's recovered enough to start work on the next Backstreet album, released to coincide with their next world tour in 1999.

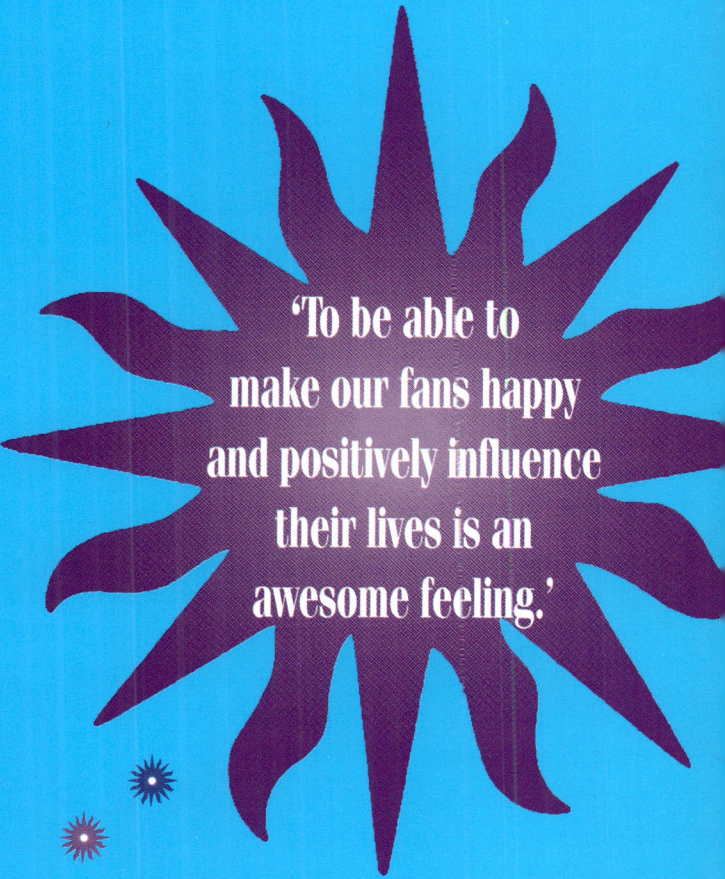

'To be able to make our fans happy and positively influence their lives is an awesome feeling.'

Like Kevin, Brian was brought up by a deeply religious family and never misses church on Sunday if he can help it. Before the band goes on stage, they and their management team always form a circle and hold hands while Brian says a prayer thanking God for their talent, health, success and fans. He also believes that God was watching over him during his health scare. 'I believe God has blessed me and left me on this earth after I was so sick as a kid so that I can make other people feel good. To be able to make our fans happy and positively influence their lives is an awesome feeling.'

He doesn't have a girlfriend but hopes, one day, to find a perfect girl who isn't fazed by his superstardom, someone to share his life — and the king-sized water bed he bought for $50.

Damon Albarn

Shy and soft-spoken in interviews, Damon Albarn really comes to life when he's on stage with Blur.

He's renowned for his boundless energy, and he once made headlines by jumping head-first into the audience stark naked!

Not satisfied just with pop stardom, the Essex-born singer recently landed the role of an East End gangster in the movie Face, which also starred Robert Carlyle. Damon got some pretty good reviews, not surprising when you consider he studied drama in London after he left school. Once, in order to research a role, Damon was forced to spend a week dressed as a secretary, in high heels, skirt and make up. It was a week he would rather forget.

Damon lives with his girlfriend, Elastica star Justine Frischmann, in London's trendy Notting Hill, but he also owns a flat and a part share in a bar in Rekyavik, the capital of Iceland. He says it's ideal for getting away from the stress of London life — and probably for avoiding the embarrassment of failing his driving test too many times! He says he's beginning to think that the examiners have it in for him just because he's famous.

Good-looking in a just-got-out-of-bed way, Damon is a reluctant sex symbol, and one who really doesn't mind what people think of him.

> Once Damon was forced to spend a week dressed as a secretary, in high heels, skirt and make up.

Rather than touring again, he and the band took most of the summer off to watch the World Cup, only leaving the sofa to play to 100,000 people in the mud and rain of the Glastonbury festival.

Lee Brennan

He's dated Baby Spice and Corrie's Jane Danson (who plays Leanne Battersby) and he's even had Mel B trying to debag him.

The hunky 911 star keeps his private life under wraps these days, but he admits there's one dream girl he'd love to chat up, and that's Louise — although he won't get the chance now she's Mrs Jamie Redknapp.

Lee has always had an eye for the ladies. He even dated a 30-year-old from his home town of Carlisle in Scotland when he was just a teenager. He says he fell in love for the first time then, but in the end she called it off because her mates kept on about him being a toy boy!

These days he just wants to find someone special — and they've got to be shorter than the 5ft 4ins star. He's said he's looking for somebody a bit smaller than him, with a nice personality, who likes him for himself — not just because he's a pop star.

He may get over 300 letters each week from fans who

These days he just wants to find someone special – and they've got to be shorter than the 5ft 4ins star.

think he is perfect, but there's one part of his body Lee hates — his feet. At seven he was happy to twinkle his toes in bright red tap shoes, but nowadays he keeps them hidden.

Lee is known for his ever-ready smile and says he's been constantly happy since beating a deadly cancer twice. He contracted Hodgkinson's disease when he was just eight years old, when his weight dropped to $2\frac{1}{2}$ stone and he was confined to a wheelchair. He recovered, but the cancer, which affects the glands, struck a second time when he was 14. 'I'm clear now, but having cancer changed my life.

It made me determined to succeed and never, never, ever give up.'

Leonardo DiCaprio

The day a pregnant Mrs DiCaprio felt her baby kick while she was gazing at an old painting by Leonardo da Vinci, she knew he was going to be very special.

So she called him Leonardo, and as soon as he could speak she got him acting — he played his first role as a three-year-old in the American TV series *Romper Room*. Fast forward 20 years and 12 movies and, thanks to *Titanic*, he's the world's hottest star. They're crazy for Leo in Japan, where girls honour him with 'Leonardo Cry Parties', and the keen bosses of Orica credit cards recently paid him £2.5 million for making a one-minute telly ad. One thing's for sure, the golden boy of the silver screen will never be hard up for cash. He makes a cool $20 million for each movie, drives a car fit for a star — a silver BMW Coupé — and lives in a Hollywood mansion with his pet bearded dragon lizard.

He's also a fave with the stars, who think Leo has the best sense of humour. Johnny Depp once paid him $500 to amuse him with funny faces and jokes and play him tunes on the organ.

On the romance front, this feline-featured pretty boy has been linked with some of Hollywood's most beautiful women, including Juliette Lewis, Liv Tyler and Alicia Silverstone.

Now all the signs are that Leo's in love. In the past he has preferred to keep quiet about his real-life relationships, but now he's said to be absolutely besotted with pretty blonde model Vanessa Haydon.

He's said it was strange playing two characters who kill themselves for love. [Romeo and Jack Dawson in *Titanic*]

He doesn't want to give girls the wrong idea about what he'd do for romance!

He's now played two characters who kill themselves for love.

Kevin
Richardson

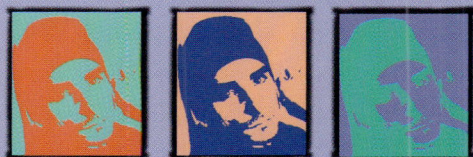

Kevin was born on a small farm in Kentucky, but grew up in a log cabin in the remote Appalachian mountains where his father ran a Christian Youth Camp.

The deeply religious lad spent most of his childhood either running free in the mountains with his pet cat Quincy, or teaching himself to play piano in the camp hall. At school, he was torn between his love of sports — he played for the American football team — and music. After seeing the Tom Cruise movie *Top Gun* he signed up to join the Air Force with dreams of becoming a pilot. But just before he was about to start training, he starred in the school musical and had girls falling at his feet. After becoming a fully qualified ballroom dance instructor he asked the Air Force to delay his training, but when they said no he gave up his ambition to fly the skies and moved to Florida where he got a job at Disney's MGM Studios, playing a Ninja Turtle and Aladdin.

It was lucky for the band, because that's where Kevin was spotted and asked to join the group.

He's had two long-term girlfriends, Christi Ore and cheerleader Kristy Flynn, but is now single. And he's not happy about it! He admits he's a shy guy who finds it hard to meet girls, and he says that when he does he worries too much about what he should say and what girls think of him. If he finally plucks up the courage to talk to someone, Kevin will make a great husband.

He makes no secret of the fact that one day he intends to settle down somewhere and raise a family.

> Just before he was about to start Air Force training, he starred in the school musical and had girls falling at his feet.

Jamie Theakston

With his seriously cute looks, fab 6ft 4ins body and super-cool interviewing techniques on *The O Zone, Live And Kicking* and *Top Of The Pops*, you'd think Jamie Theakston would have had more girlfriends than hot dinners.

But it's a shock to discover that All Saints star Natalie Appleton is only his third girlfriend. He admits he used to play around a lot with one-night-stands, but he found it really unfulfilling. He reckons he spent nearly three years looking for the right girlfriend — now he thinks he's found her.

He's said he's still flattered that Nat hasn't gone off him yet. If she does dump him, there'll be queues around the block for the best-dressed man on telly. But he's not just cute on the outside. He admits to being an incurable romantic, giving presents like books of poetry and flowers, and if you're invited round to Jamie's for dinner, be prepared for a gourmet feast. He can't keep out of the kitchen, and loves cooking romantic dinners for two.

> He reckons he spent nearly three years looking for the right girlfriend – now he thinks he's found her.

Jamie says his stable upbringing on a farm near Brighton has helped him keep his feet on the ground. He lives alone in a tiny flat in London's Notting Hill and when he's not working keeps away from the razzle of showbusiness, listening to music and playing footie with his mate Robbie Williams.

'I'm not into all that showbiz stuff. Relationships with my family and friends are more important to me than celebrity parties.

I'd much rather kick a football around Hyde Park than go to some movie premiere.'

Matt Le Blanc

You could spend hours listing Matt Le Blanc's best qualities: the bee-stung lips, high cheekbones, sleepy brown doe eyes, impossibly white teeth, floppy fringe and rippling pecs.

With all his desirable qualities it's hardly surprising there's millions of girls on the planet who want to superglue themselves to the *Friend*'s babe-magnet.

But there's only one woman in Matt's life... his mum. He freely admits he's a mummy's boy, devoted to his much-loved mother Pat, who struggled working shifts in a factory to bring up her boy alone while his dad was off fighting in the Vietnam war.

Matt met his dad for the first time when he was eight — the same year he got his first motorbike. He started racing in competitions, but when he decided on a career as a professional rider he ran into a major roadblock — his mum, who decided her only son needed a safer outlet for his talents. He stopped racing, but couldn't give up his love of dangerous sports — he's now a snowboarding and ski-diving freak.

After graduating from school, he left his hometown of Newton, Massachusetts and moved to New York, where he stacked shelves in a supermarket and worked in a burger bar until he was spotted in the street by a modelling scout. Adverts for Heinz ketchup, Coca-Cola and as the Levi's 501 man followed, until he got his first break on the American TV series *TV 101* and moved to Los Angeles. Two years later he won the role of the dim but hunky womanizer in *Friends*. Matt admits he's been a bit of a womanizer in real-life too. He's dated Goldie Hawn's 16-year-old daughter Camille Cerio, actress Minnie Driver, *Friends* co-star Jennifer Aniston and even Amanda de Cadenet. But he says he's decided to look for a steady girlfriend now he's turned 30.

He's also recently starred in his first role in a major movie, *Lost In Space,* where he plays the hero who battles against Gary Oldman's baddie to save the Robinson family.

> He's decided to look for a steady girlfriend now he's turned 30

19

Aaron Carter

Born on 7th December 1987 – just one minute after his twin sister Angel – Aaron is the last of the Carter clan.

It was obvious when he was just a wee young lad that he would follow the footsteps of his famous brother, Backstreet Boy Nick. He was only seven when he formed his first band, Dead End, with three of his classmates from Rock School in Florida. The group split in 1996, due to differing tastes in music, but it was probably the best thing that happened to Aaron because he honed his talent with a voice coach and went on to cut his first solo single, 'Crush On You'.

The turning point in his life came when, during a special appearance at a Backstreet Boys concert in 1997, a record company exec caught his act and signed him on the spot. 'It was the best moment of my life when I went on stage with the Backstreet Boys. All the girls were chanting my name and it was like "Whoah!" I'd never felt anything like it in the world. It was fantastic.' He's very close to big brother Nick and the pair are always competing — at the moment they're seeing who can collect the most and rarest Beanie Baby toys. Wherever he goes in the world, he hits the toy shops looking for Beanie Babies that Nick hasn't got.

Aaron admits to being a bit too young — he's only 10 and 4'6" short — to be seriously dating. He did fancy a girl in his last video, but he won't say who! He says he wishes he had time for a girlfriend, but when he's not working he can usually be found in front of a computer screen or practising his saxophone.

For a schoolboy, Aaron — whose dad Bob calls him Airboy — certainly packs plenty into his busy life. He often visits three continents in as many weeks when he's on the road promoting his records, and he reckons the only thing that keeps him going is Coca Cola and Pringles crisps.

> 'It was the best moment of my life when I went on stage with the Backstreet Boys.'

He's certainly the only pop star whose hand can fit perfectly into the bottom of a Pringles tube!

Michael Owen

England and Liverpool star striker Michael Owen has a lot to live up to.

As a schoolboy he scored a record-breaking 97 goals in one season, he is the youngest player ever to play for England, and his amazing goal against Argentina in France 98 was hailed as one of the best in World Cup history. The 18-year-old has vowed to stick with Liverpool, despite being courted by some of Europe's top teams. Unusually for a footballer, he has quickly gained nearly as many female fans as male, due as much to his cheeky grin as his silky skills. Almost overnight he has taken over from David Beckham as Britain's sexiest soccer star — he was mobbed when he visited his old school in Hawarden, and fan club sites have sprung up across the Internet. He's said he's not bothered by the attention he's getting, although he finds it flattering, and he's refused to cash in on his footballing success by signing huge sponsorship deals, preferring to concentrate on his on-pitch activities. But what does he do for fun? Like fellow stars Robbie Williams and Chris Evans, Michael enjoys a round of golf with his team-mates, although he admits he's not quite as skilled on the golf course as he is on the football pitch.

Michael has been seen relaxing this summer on holiday with his model girlfriend Louise. The two were childhood sweethearts, but he insists that marriage isn't really on the agenda at his age. Michael is having a house built just a mile from his parents' home in Cheshire, which will have five bedrooms and a snooker room, another of his favourite sports. But Louise won't be moving in with him for the time being.

He has quickly gained nearly as many female fans as male, due as much to his cheeky grin as his silky skills.

This sensible teenager always keeps his feet on the ground except when he's putting another **blinding** goal in the back of the net.

Matthew Marsden

It's odds on that the 6ft 4ins hunk with twinkling blue eyes will fulfil his latest ambition – to be a world-famous singer. After all, Matt's already been a successful model, film actor and top TV soap star. He played dishy Danny Weir in *Emmerdale* for five months and a transvestite in the French film *Les Soeurs Soleil,* but it was as *Coronation Street's* hard man Chris Collins that he made his name. The steamy story lines saw him have an affair with Sally, a punch up with her jealous hubby Kevin, and then the randy mechanic was at it again – caught between the duvet and the sheet with barmaid Sam by furious fiance Des Barnes. His acting won him the Best Newcomer gong at the National TV Awards, but everyone thought his career had taken a wrong turn when he decided to leave The Street and concentrate on his singing. But it didn't take long for the man who shares Michelle Gayle's singing coach to hit the charts around the world and become an overnight pop god.

But what about Matt's private life? Last year he split from girlfriend Rachel and, very surprisingly, he's still single. He says he was spoiled when he was modelling because he was surrounded by amazing looking women. And they seem like him too: he turned down the chance of escorting Madonna to the 1998 Brit Awards, after the star saw some pics of him. He learned to cope with life in the fast lane of showbiz success by becoming a Buddhist, and wears a Ninja tattoo on his ankle, a Japanese symbol meaning 'To be different and to excel'.

He turned down the chance of escorting Madonna to the 1998 Brit Awards

He's said that he wants another tattoo, of a particular sort of dragon, but now he's gutted because All Saints' Mel beat him to it.

Nick Carter

Believe it or not, Nick Carter was just a cute little 11-year-old when he was picked to join the Backstreet Boys line-up. Before that, the multi-talented youngster had won a few small acting roles, including one in the hit Johnny Depp movie *Edward Scissorhands*.

But his early success meant that he had a tough time at school, where the older boys picked on him for doing showbiz things.

So, the day he joined Backstreet — named after the mall in Orlando where the boys used to hang-out — Nick happily dropped out of his school. For the six years he's been in the band he's had a private tutor on tour to help him with his studies, but even though he admits it solved the problem of being bullied, he says that it can still be a real pain. When the other guys are having a lie-in, he has to get up and do schoolwork.

Nick's experiences at his school in Tampa, Florida,

where his mum Jane and dad Bob run a retirement home, left a marked impression on him when it comes to girls. He says that he had crushes on some girls when he was at school, but they weren't interested in him because he wasn't one of the cool guys. He's said that the girls he was friends with at school weren't necessarily the pretty ones, but they were good on the inside. It made a big impact on the way he looks at girls now. 'I'm not interested in somebody just 'cos they look like some gorgeous model. I look for a good heart in a girl before I care about how they look.'

Any potential girlfriend needs to have good sea legs because Nick's favourite pastime is to drive his parents' motor boat to a quiet spot on the Gulf Of Mexico and go scuba diving.

And when he's drying off in the sun there's nothing he likes better than drawing comic book characters.

> 'I look for a good heart in a girl before I care about how they look.'

Rich

Neville

On the face of it, Richard Neville has everything a bloke could ever want; he's handsome, talented and a member of one of Britain's best bands. But there's one thing missing from his life – a girlfriend. And he says it's doing his head in. 'I want a girlfriend so badly. I'd always had a girlfriend since I was in primary school. But joining Five has completely killed my love life. We're never in one place long enough to meet anybody. I've only really fallen head-over-heels in love once and that was when I was 16. I'll never forget it. We were together for a year, but we started arguing and split up. I've been looking for the same sort of feeling ever since.'

Rich, who grew up in Bromsgrove, Birmingham, has a clear idea of his perfect date. 'I love the winter when I can get cosy on a big rug by the fire with a girl. I'm not feeling sorry for myself, but the rate things are going I'll be an old man before I get the chance to live out my dream.'

He went to one of Britain's poshest public schools, but he never liked academic work. 'I found schoolwork quite hard and I had awful handwriting, then I discovered I

'It was one of the best days of my life joining Five. A dream come true.'

had dyslexia. Being dyslexic probably accounts for why I've always loved music and acting.

The other guys in the band always take the mick out of me about my musical tastes. I know it's not cool but I'm not ashamed to admit it – I'm a huge fan of any music by Barbara Streisand and Neil Diamond.'

Rich – who wants to be an actor one day – became a member of the National Youth Theatre at 14, and wowed the audience at the Edinburgh Festival with his role in the play *Body Work,* but it was his singing and dancing talents that won him the job with Five.

'It was one of the best days of my life joining Five. A dream come true. We've done things I never thought would ever be possible – like having a hit record in America and touring the world. In fact the past year has been incredible. The only down point has been England going out of the World Cup. I'm a huge football fan and I really believed we were going to win.

I was so gutted when we lost that I cried.'

Ewan McGregor

He is probably Britain's sexiest and most successful movie star, but Ewan McGregor still can't believe his good fortune: 'On the scale of things, in this business, I've been the luckiest man alive. Sometimes I go in my bathroom, shut the door and jump up and down like an excited five-year-old. And as for the reaction I get from women, well, I've never been so flattered in my life.'

After he starred as bad boy Renton in the cult film *Trainspotting*, Ewan couldn't walk down the street without getting mobbed by girls. But you'll never spot him leaving swanky nightclubs with different girls on his arm because he's a married man with a kid. But that hasn't put off any of his fans who've caught sight of his naked body in movies like *The Pillow Book* or *Velvet Goldmine*. 'I don't have a problem with taking my clothes off.'

These days he's an A-list Hollywood star, but it wasn't long ago that he was a little boy growing up in a remote part of Scotland, where he mucked out the stable every weekend just to get the chance to ride the horses. Ewan spent every summer running wild in the hills and forests. 'I was a naughty boy. Me and my mates would spend all day with our catapults getting up to no good. I loved every minute of it.'

He'd wanted to be an actor since the age of nine and would spend all weekend and most evenings watching his favourite black and white movies on telly.

But it was his uncle — Local Hero star Denis Lawson — who really made Ewan want to act. 'He'd come to our house in his Afghan coat and beads with no shoes on his feet and I thought, "Yeah, that's what I want to be."' At 16, he was always in trouble at school, so he left the school where his dad was a teacher without a job or any prospects. A week later he was working backstage at the Perth Repertory Theatre, a job which eventually led to acting stardom.

'I don't have a problem with taking my clothes off.'

AJ McLean

Nicknamed Bone because he's so thin, Alex – or AJ – certainly made an impression when he auditioned for the band as a 14-year-old.

They were all knocked out by his natural rhythm, great voice and abundance of confidence and picked him as the first Backstreet Boy. Mind you, he was used to performing – he had been modelling, singing and dancing since he was seven, and he worked as a puppeteer on the Nickelodeon show *Welcome Freshman*.

He admits that the pressure of being a Backstreet Boy occasionally gets to him, and he sometimes even sits and cries in his room because he wants to go back home to Orlando, Florida. However, he says that the thrill he gets on stage from hearing the fans makes up for any lonely moments.

Backstreet have won umpteen awards and today spend most of their life on the road wowing their millions of fans around the world. AJ admits that the band meet so many people that it can be hard to remember people's names, but he never forgets a girl's name. And surprisingly for a man whose sunglasses are his trade mark, the first thing AJ looks for in a girl is beautiful eyes. She'd also have to be a shopaholic, like him; AJ likes nothing better than to shop until he can't fit any more bags in his car. These days he's used to hearing girls scream for him, but his first girlfriend dumped him because he told lies.

> AJ likes nothing better than to shop until he can't fit any more bags in his car.

Looking back he thinks he looked like a nerd at school, because he used to wear glasses – even though his sight is perfect – because he thought it looked cool.

Robbie Williams

His fame, talent and extraordinary looks mean that he gets more than his fair share of female attention.

Take That made Robbie a very rich young man indeed, but he hated the 'boy band' image.
In the summer of 1995 he rebelled, arriving at the Glastonbury festival in a limo full of champagne to find his freedom and hang out with Oasis. He soon started doing drugs and getting so drunk that he'd happily risk his neck with death-wish stunts like hanging out of a speeding car and leaping from first floor windows. For 16 months after he left Take That Robbie admits he was so out of it he didn't know what he was doing. He put on weight and made some embarassing TV appearances, and was taunted by the press with names like Blobbie Robbie and Yobbie Robbie. But a new slimline and straight Robbie emerged to win a whole new audience with his anthemic single 'Angels'. His fame, talent and extraordinary looks mean that he gets more than his fair share of female attention: he's been linked with Anna Friel, Natalie Imbruglia, Denise Van Outen and The Hon Jacqui Hamilton-Smith, and he most recently fell for All Saint Nicky Appleton. Although the path of love has been rocky for Nic and Rob, he went down on one knee before his Albert Hall gig at the end of his sell-out tour and proposed marriage, and Nicky's now wearing his massive emerald-cut diamond ring. Robbie's first album *Life Thru a Lens* went quadruple-platinum, and judging by the success of the single 'Millennium' the new one will do even better.

Not bad for the boy from Stoke who first made his living selling double-glazing.

35

Ronan Keating

An international superstar at the age of 21, Ronan Keating has done a lot of growing up in the five years since he joined Boyzone.

Brought up in a poor district of Dublin, the youngest of five children, Ronan was first encouraged to follow his musical dreams by his mother. Since she passed away early in 1998, Ronan has had a hard time adjusting, and he says that he will never forget her.

He's said that his mother was his best friend in the whole world, and that he still talks to her in his prayers whenever he can.

But there have been some great times this year as well. His marriage to his new wife Yvonne on the Caribbean island of Nevis was the surprise showbiz wedding of the year, although it was a disappointment for besotted fans as another of the Boyz took the plunge.

At school, Ronan admits he was pretty bad at academic work. He loved reading and writing poetry though, and his literary skills have been useful when it comes to songwriting. This year he won a prestigious Ivor Novello award for the Boyzone track 'Picture of You'.

Ronan has said that although he's adjusted to the fact that he's now a millionaire, there are very few places rather than Dublin that he'd rather live. And he's not too worried about what will happen when his years with Boyzone come to an end.

His marriage was the surprise showbiz wedding of the year.

He's said that if his jetset lifestyle fell to pieces tomorrow and he lost everything, his life would be far from over.

He and Yvonne would be quite happy to get a little caravan on a beach in Mexico and live there for the rest of their lives.

David
Schwimmer

Friends **star David went to Beverley Hills High School, made famous by the hit show** Beverley Hills 90210.

But he wasn't like the super-cool dudes in the TV series. Rather than hanging out in trendy coffee bars and at parties with beautiful women, he reckons he was always the class geek, staying in and working. He's said it made him feel like a loser.

Today the sexy Mr Nice of telly receives marriage proposals, knickers and nude pictures through the post from fans. But he's said that he can never get used to the fact that he's a sex symbol. He was tall, skinny and painfully shy at school and had to wear braces for 12 hours a day. No wonder he says he never got the girl at school.

Mind you, he's made up for lost time since bagging his role in Friends, dating the lovely Natalie Imbruglia for a year before the pressure of their work schedules drove them apart. He's said that being in a series like Friends is hard on his private life — it's almost impossible for him to meet someone who has never seen him on TV. He admits his biggest problem is chatting girls up — he says he feels gawky and stupid, like he was back at school again.

David had a true Hollywood childhood, growing up in a million-dollar mansion with his top LA lawyer parents. His mum specializes in divorces and handled Roseanne Barr's first marriage split, so David learned first-hand how easy it is to end up in marriage hell.

Not that he'd have time for a family.

He was tall, skinny and painfully shy at school and had to wear braces for 12 hours a day.

He has a three-picture deal with Miramax Films, earns over £60,000 per episode of *Friends* and is signed to stay with the show until the year 2000.

39

Shane Lynch

They must put something magical in the water because there's three pop stars in the Lynch household.

After five years topping the charts around the world, Boyzone star Shane now has his sisters, B*witched twins Edele and Keavy, sharing his limelight. It's lucky that Shane isn't the jealous type — instead he's said that he's proud that his sisters had a number one hit with their first single.

Shane comes from a very close-knit Dublin family and, as the only boy in a family with five sisters, he learned early on what it takes to get along with women. In fact, he admits that the only time he ever lost his temper with his sisters was when his pet snake Caesar died after they forgot to feed him. Growing up with so many girls around him was probably why he plucks one of his eyebrows — he picked up their talent for grooming. Shane's honest when it comes to love. Most men's idea of the perfect romantic gesture is buying flowers and dinner, but Shane would rather take a girl car racing! 'In relationships, I think you should take things slowly. I might kiss a girl on a first date if things went very well, but then again I might not. I certainly wouldn't go any further than that.'

It was his respect for the opposite sex that attracted Eternal star Easther, who became Shane's wife following their secret wedding ceremony in Essex earlier this year. 'I definitely want to be a dad. I want to have at least six kids and more boys than girls.

'I might kiss a girl on a first date if things went very well, but then again, I might not.'

I have five sisters, so I would want more boy power in my family.'

Howie Dorough

Howard Dwaine Dorough, or Howie D, inherited his sexy Latin looks from his Puerto Rican mum Paula.

But it wasn't his pin-up appearance that won the hearts of every girl at his school in Orlando, Florida — it was his sweet singing voice. He once sang 'Unchained Melody' at a talent show in front of 800 pupils and teachers, reducing many of them to tears.

The 24-year-old, who's nicknamed Latin Lover and Sweet D because he loves talking to girls, admits he drives the other guys and his security guards crazy because he spends such a long time signing autographs and chatting to fans. They always threaten to drive off without me. But they haven't done yet! I love talking to our fans — in fact I can never get enough of them.'

He also spends most of his time with the band looking through the lens of a video camera. He's got some really embarrassing footage of the guys over the years, so he's got plenty of material to blackmail them should they ever step out of line!

Howie started acting at six after one of his three sisters got him to play a munchkin in a production of *The Wizard Of Oz*, and has appeared in the movies *Cop And A Half* and Steve Martin's hit comedy *Parenthood*. He works hard to keep his body perfect, and it's a well-known fact that he never goes to bed without doing his push-ups and stomach crunches. When they're abroad, the rest of the band always head to the nearest MacDonalds, but not Howie — wherever he is he seeks out local healthy food.

That is, if he can remember where he's going. Howie has the worse memory and sense of direction and is forever getting lost. He has such a bad memory that he's thinking of buying a mini-computer to organize his life.

'I love talking to our fans – in fact I can never get enough of them'

Perhaps he should get a homing device too, so the other guys will be able to find him!

43

Taylor Hanson

Although Taylor Hanson loves making music and playing live, the Hanson rise to fame has meant that his life has become a constant whirl of interviews, gigs and travel.

'We never get a day off. If I did I would just like to lay around, pig out and watch movies.' He's the brother who gets most attention from Hanson's female fans — people have said that he looks like a young Kurt Cobain — but he insists that people judge him on the music he makes rather than his looks. His gorgeous blond hair is a result of his Danish ancestors, and he gets his talent from the family's musical upbringing in Tulsa, Oklahoma. He describes himself as the professional in the band, and has said he would love to meet his pop idol Michael Jackson. However, he doesn't want Hanson to be compared to hugely successful bands like The Jackson Five, preferring to wait and see what the future holds. Tay plays keyboards, tambourine and sings lead vocals,

'We never get a day off. If I did I would just like to lay around, pig out and watch movies.'

but his abilities don't end there. He draws wild cartoons whenever he gets the creative urge, and has painted murals on the walls of his parents' garage.

What really makes Taylor mad is critics suggesting that because they are so young, Hanson don't really play their instruments or write their own songs.

'A lot of people have asked us, "Why are you in a band when you're so young?" and we say, "Well what are we meant to do? Wait until we're 21 before we start making music?"

We couldn't just not make the music.'

44

Will Mellor

Determined not to be seen as just another soap star turned pop singer, *Hollyoaks* heart-throb Will insists his own compositions are featured as extra tracks on his singles, and always sings live.

But Will has a dark secret from his past — he was the singer in a failed boy band! Called Right Now, they never even got a record contract and even Will has described them as ropey. He's sure someone will find photos of the band and try to blackmail him!

As a result of playing crazy singer Jambo in *Hollyoaks*, record companies were clamouring to sign him up for a solo deal — with some desperation. He says that some of them even offered him recording contracts without even hearing him sing.

He insisted on releasing as his first single a cover of an old Leo Sayer hit, 'When I Need You', as a tribute to his disabled sister Joanne — it's her favourite song. Will encountered tabloid trouble early in 1998, when the papers accused him of two-timing girlfriend Angela Griffin (Fiona Middleton in *Coronation Street*). Will admitted he'd been seeing fellow pop star Shola Ama, but after begging forgiveness from Angela — and giving her a £2000 Cartier watch — the couple were reunited. Will's even talking to the tabloids again now!

He's a rather different character to the one he plays on TV, but he's just as hungry as Jambo to hit the big time. There's no doubt in Will's mind where his future lies.

He's vowed that if his music career takes off he'll have to give up acting — which will be bad news for *Hollyoaks* fans.

> Will has a dark secret from his past – he was once the singer in a failed boy band.

BOY POWER

FUJI RDPII

Picture Credits

All Action
Doug Peters: 10, 47
Nick Tansley: 26

Alpha
Mark Allan: 42

Famous
Casper: 15, 27, 35, 36, 37, 40, 41
Hubert Boesl: 19, 31
Kurt Krieger: 12, 39
Rob Howard: 29
Ralph Ottis: 21

LFI
Andrew Catlin: 8
Greg DeGuire: 44
David Fisher: 17, 24
Lawrence Marano: 45
Ilpo Musto: 15

Kobal Collection:
Kobal Collection: 13

Redferns
Paul Bergen: 6
Kieran Docherty: 34
Jill Douglas: 46
JM Enternational: 7
Michael Linssen: 4, 5, 28, 32
Mick Hutson: 9

Retna
Roslyn Gaunt: 11
Rob Hann: 30
B. Khan: 33

Rex
Eva Magazine: 16
Nick Johnston/Sunday Magazine: 25
Brian Rasic: 20
Rex: 18, 38, 43
Tim: 22, 23

**The Publishers would like
to thank the following for
their permission to use
quotes in the book:**
Big Magazine: 20, 44 (left)
Live and Kicking Magazine: 11, 16
© The Guardian: 4 [Caroline Sullivan], 44
(right) [Michael Bracewell]
Rob McGibbon: 7, 27, 43
Smash Hits: 40